The Wok Cookbook

Delicious And Filling Chinese Recipes To Enjoy

RONNIE ISRAEL

ISBN-13:978-1516883493

ISBN-10:1516883497

DEDICATION

To all those who love to cook

TABLE OF CONTENTS

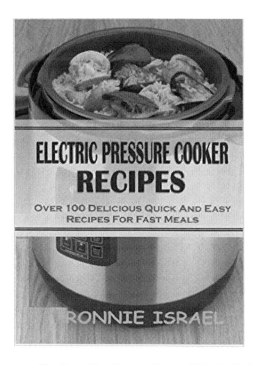

Electric Pressure Cooker Recipes: Over 100 Delicious Quick And Easy Recipes For Fast Meals

INTRODUCTION

The wok has been used for centuries in Asia and has become a vital kitchen utensil in the West, having been exported by Chinese immigrants for over a hundred years. The wok is a large thin metal pan with a bowl-like shape with one or two wooden handles. It has a diameter of about 14 inches and a slightly flat bottom.

Woks are indispensable for cooking authentic great-tasting oriental dishes. It has been said that if you are not coking in a wok, you aren't doing Asian cooking. It is the traditional kitchen utensil for stir-frying. Besides its original purpose of stir-frying however, the wok can also be used for steaming, braising, deep-frying, searing, sautéing, stewing and poaching. Its versatility is simply mind-blowing. Just one wok and you can make thousands of recipes.

The best woks are made of carbon steel and can be used on a stove or an electric gas. Woks transfer all the heat directly from the flame to the food. The average temperature of a wok is usually very hot— from 320°F to more than 446°F. As a result, meats get cooks as soon as it is placed in the pan, retaining the good juices and absorbing the fat, however little.

New woks always have a layer (you may or may not see it) which must be rubbed off. Use a hard scourer, liquid detergent and hot water to do this. Dry the wok with a paper towel. The next process is to season your wok. Seasoning involves burning a natural non-stick layer into the pan to prevent food from sticking to its bottom and to avoid rust.

Here are 5 basic steps to seasoning a new wok:

1. Keep your kitchen well ventilated and then place the wok over high heat. It will start to smoke within 5 seconds. Tilt the wok over the flame for about a minute so it can be well heated. A yellow or blue ring will now form. Remove wok from flame and leave to cool for 30 seconds.

2. Grease the inside of the wok with a piece of kitchen towel that has been soaked with oil. Heat the wok over low heat and tilt around for 30 seconds. Remove from flame.

3. Wipe the wok clean and dry with a kitchen towel. Now repeat step 2.

4. Let the wok cool down for a while and then wash it a soft sponge and hot water. Do not use washing-up liquid. Heat it under a low flame again for 1-2 minutes. When it cools down, grease it again slightly with oil and a paper towel.

5. Your wok is seasoned and now ready for use.

Stir-Frying

Stir-frying is the most popular of all Asian cooking methods. It is simply the rapid frying of small cuts of ingredients in a little bit of oil over intense heat. The process involves tossing, stirring and/or mixing the ingredients which often comprise of meat, fish and/or vegetables. The high temperature and short cooking time ensure that the nutrient and taste of each food ingredient are retained.

A wok's round shape makes it easy to stir-fry. Pushing the ingredients up against the sides ensures that they keep falling back to the middle of the pan where the heat is. Stir-fried meals are well seasoned; they cook evenly and quickly and are also delicious and healthy. Electric woks do not retain heat well so they aren't suitable for stir-frying. However, they are perfect for braising, poaching, stewing and steaming.

It is also important to stir-fry ingredients in their appropriate order. Vegetables that are slow-cooking should be added first, e.g. celery or carrots before quick- cooking veggies like tomatoes or bean sprouts. Preparation is essential. Stir-frying is quick cooking; there is no time to start chopping and cutting once you start cooking. Ingredients must be chopped, sliced and/or grated before you start to cook. These ingredients must also be within reach. Ensure that the cut vegetables and other ingredients are even in size and shape.

Most recipes require peanut or sesame oil but less saturated oil such as corn oil or canola can be used. Do not use butter or margarine for stir-frying because they have a low smoke point. Oil's smoke point is the temperature when a fat dissolves, gives off smoke and produces a greasy taste and pleasant smell. Heat the oil to a high temperature before you add the food ingredients. However, ensure it is not smoking. Vegetables stir- fried this way remain crisp and tender and still retain their color.

A little oil is required for fish and vegetables as long as the wok has been well seasoned. Pour the oil in a swirling motion along the wok's edge and as the oil slides down along the edges, other pre-cut ingredients should be added quickly.

Stir- frying has lots of advantages over other types of cooking methods. Some of them include:

- Stir frying requires small amounts of oil, especially when compared to deep-fat frying. This leads to less fat and fewer calories added.
- Vegetables retain more vitamins and minerals when stir-fried than when boiled. Boiling causes the loss of water-soluble vitamins.
- Stir frying reduces waste by using small amounts of fresh vegetables from the refrigerator.
- Stir-frying saves time since meals are prepared quickly. Less time is also used for clean-up since the meals are made in one pan.
- The use of different kinds of vegetables makes it easier to use smaller amounts of poultry, meats or seafood which helps to save up on grocery.

Wok Cooking Tips To Remember

Have your ingredients at hand so you can work fast when ready to cook. Marinate your meat, finely cut vegetables and have the spices within reach. Use peanut oil if available as it can tolerate strong heat. Other oils that can also be used include maize oil, rice oil, soybeans oil and sunflower oil. Olive oil is less suitable.

Ensure that the pan is the right temperature by pouring a few drops of water in it. If it gives off small sizzling bubbles, this shows that the wok is at the right temperature. The next step is to add a little oil. Once it begins to smell slightly, this shows it is hot enough for use. The oil must also cover all the sides of the wok.

Do not put too much in the pan all at once. This action lowers the temperature of the wok and leaves you stewing the ingredients instead of stir-frying them. If possible, remove the meat and the fish from the pan for a little while and add it again towards the end. This way, it will not be overdone.

The Chinese Kitchen

Using fresh ingredients is the starting point of oriental cooking. Fresh ingredients retain more nutrients and juices when it comes under high cooking temperature. Here are a few sauces and vegetables that commonly occur in many Asian recipes.

Peanut oil

Peanut oil contains significantly less fat compared to sunflower oil. While it doesn't have a strong aroma, it is slightly more refined in taste. This means, it is great for preparing mild dressings and mayonnaise. However, peanut oil is the best for stir-frying and deep-frying.

Tofu

Also known as bean curd, Tofu is a popular Chinese staple. Tofu is made from pureed soybean milk and is high in protein, and low in calories. It has a smooth texture but a bland flavor which enables it go well with other foods.

Ginger

Ginger root adds a distinctive sharp flavor to Chinese dishes. Besides being used in cooking, fresh ginger can also be used for making tea. It has a medicinal effect and can provide remedies for nausea, stomach ache and nausea. Powdered ginger is not as flavorful as the fresh ones but ½ teaspoon of powdered ginger can be substituted for 1 teaspoon of minced fresh ginger or for 2 slices of fresh ginger.

Spring Onion

Spring onions add a subtle, fresh flavor to dishes. Spring onions taste well in salads, meat, fish and egg dishes as well. Steam the rings quickly, if you intend to do so as they lose their flavor quickly.

Sesame Oil

Sesame oil is rich in flavor. It is pressed from sesame seeds that has been peeled and roasted. The cold-pressed, western sesame oil is ideal for frying with.

Thai Basil

Thai basil are cut into strips and added to wok dishes, soups and curries at the last moment. There are three main types:

Lemon basil– is often added to salad and fish dishes.

Thai "holy" basil – it has slightly hairy leaves and taste really light.

Thai "sweet" basil – it has a strong taste similar to aniseed and a little like mint

Bok Choy

Bok Choy is the most widely consumed vegetable in China. It has dark-green leaves, flexible crunchy white stems and a slight mustard taste. The large bok choy is usually stir-fried, boiled or steamed for a few minutes. The stems are added first and the leaves at the last minute. The small type, baby bok choy, can be cooked whole in the wok by steaming or boiling. It tastes great in soups and salads.

Soy Sauce

Soy sauce, a combination of flour, soybeans, salt and water is a common seasoning in many recipes. It is salty so there is no need to ask more salt to the recipes. It is usually added for flavor at the last minute of cooking. There is the dark soy sauce, which has a more syrupy texture and is less salty than the regular soy sauce. It even tastes a little sweet. Darker soy sauces are usually used to add color to hot meals such as stews and braised beef. Keep soy sauce bottles tightly closed when not in use and stored in the refrigerator to help retain flavor

Five-Spice Powder

This Chinese spice is a mixture of five basic flavors (sharp, salty, sweet, bitter and sour). These flavors are usually found in cloves, fennel seeds, Szechuan pepper, Chinese cinnamon, cloves and star anise. Five-spice powder is often rubbed into pork and duck before the meats are toasted or fried. However, it should be used in small quantity because of its intense taste.

Szechuan Pepper

Named after the Chinese region of Szechuan, Szechuan pepper has slight lemon flavor. This spice, though not a real pepper, has a small numbing effect on the tongue. It is often used in fish dishes, and sometimes in chicken, rabbit and veal dishes as well.

CHICKEN RECIPES

Chicken-Almond Delight

Serves: 3

Enjoy this tasty meal over brown rice.

Ingredients

3 large chicken breasts, boneless, skinless & cut into ½-inch cubes

2 tablespoons soy sauce

¼ cup dry sherry

1 clove garlic, smashed

1 inch fresh ginger, grated

Peanut, coconut or canola oil

½ cup slivered almonds

1½ cups snow peas, cut in half

1½ cups mushrooms, sliced

15 scallions, cut into pieces about 1 inch long

¼ cup water chestnuts, sliced, optional

Directions

1. Combine the soy sauce, garlic, sherry and ginger well.

2. Heat teaspoons of your preferred oil in a wok and add the almonds. Stir-fry until light golden. Remove from heat and set aside.

3. Heat more tablespoons of oil in the wok and add the mushrooms, snow peas, scallions and water chestnuts (if desired).

4. Stir-fry until just barely tender-crisp. Remove and set aside. Heat yet another couple of tablespoons oil in the wok and add the chicken. Stir-fry until done.

5. Return the vegetables to the wok and add the sherry/ soy sauce mixture. Toss together well.

6. Cover and simmer 4 minutes. Top with almonds and serve.

5 Minutes Chicken Stir-Fry

Serves: 4

Ingredients

2 cups of cooked chicken, cut in bite-size pieces

2 tablespoons dry sherry

3 tablespoons soy sauce

2 teaspoons cornstarch

1 tablespoon vegetable oil

¼ teaspoon ground ginger

3 cups frozen mixed oriental vegetables, thawed

1cup cold water

Directions

1. To prepare the sauce, combine water, cornstarch, soy sauce, ginger and sherry. Stir well and then set aside.

2. Pour oil in a wok and stir-fry the vegetables in it for 3-4 minutes.

3. Stir the sauce; add it to center of wok, cooking and stirring until bubbly and thickened.

4. Add the cooked chicken, stir all together. Cook 2 minutes until heated through.

5. Serve immediately.

Rotisserie Chicken Chop Suey

Serves: 4

<u>Ingredients</u>

8 packaged (3 by 3-inch) Chinese wonton skins, separated

1 tablespoon plus 2 teaspoons canola oil

2 scallions, (about 1/4 cup) greens included, trimmed & sliced thinly

3 cloves garlic, sliced

4 cups napa cabbage, sliced

1 can (8-ounce) bamboo shoots, drained& julienned

2 cups (about 6 ounces) shiitake mushrooms, cleaned, trimmed & thinly sliced

3/4 cup celery (about 2 long stalks or 4 celery hearts), thinly sliced

3/4 teaspoon sugar

1 1/2 tablespoons low-sodium soy sauce

1 cup low-sodium chicken broth

2 tablespoons toasted sesame oil

2 cups cubed or shredded cooked turkey or chicken

1 1/2 teaspoons cornstarch dissolved in 1 tablespoon cooking sherry

2 cups cooked brown rice

1/4 teaspoon salt

1 tablespoon toasted sesame seeds

<u>Directions</u>

1. Preheat oven to 375 degrees F. Lightly brush the baking sheet and the wonton skins on both sides with 2 teaspoons canola oil.

2. Sprinkle with salt and bake until browned and crisp. Remove to cool in a rack and reserve.

3. In a wok, heat the 1 tablespoon of canola oil that's left over medium-high heat.

4. Now add the garlic, cabbage, scallion, celery, mushrooms and bamboo shoots, stir-frying about 3 to 4 minutes until cabbage is soft and wilted.

5. Add 3/4 cup of the chicken broth, the sugar, sesame oil and soy sauce and cook for 3 minutes.

6. Add the cornstarch- sherry mixture and, if the mixture is a bit dry, the extra 1/4 cup of chicken stock.

7. Add the chicken and heat through. Serve over the cooked brown rice and top with reserved crushed wonton skins and sesame seeds.

8. (4 servings will yield1 cup chop suey, 1/2 cup brown rice & 2 wonton skins)

Chinese Tea Smoked Chicken

Serves: 8

<u>Ingredients</u>

1/2 cup rice

1/2 cup black Chinese tea leaves

4 whole chicken breasts, skin on

1 teaspoon Chinese five-spice powder

1 teaspoon Szechwan peppercorns

1/4 cup of freshly chopped gingerroot

1/2 cup brown sugar

<u>Directions</u>

1. Wash the chicken and pat dry. Mix together the peppercorns and five-spice powder and then rub this mixture onto the dry chicken.

2. Line the wok with aluminum foil. Add together the tea, sugar, ginger and rice in a small bowl. Place this mixture on the foil in the wok. Heat wok on medium temperature until it begins to smoke.

3. Place the chicken skin-side up on a rack, 3 inches over the tea mixture. Cover and smoke for until chicken is thoroughly cooked.

4. Remove from wok. Serve with rice and steamed vegetables, if desired.

Szechuan Chicken Stir-Fry

This flavorful stir-fry will add a little zip to your weeknight dinners.

Serves: 4

<u>Ingredients</u>

1/2 cup fat-free, lower-sodium chicken broth

1 tablespoon dark sesame oil, divided

2 tablespoons canola oil, divided

1 tablespoon rice vinegar

2 teaspoons chili paste

2 teaspoons of cornstarch

1 yellow bell pepper, cut into strips

1 pound skinless, boneless chicken breast halves, cut into bite-sized pieces

1 red bell pepper, cut into strips

1 tablespoon minced fresh garlic

2 tablespoons lower-sodium soy sauce

1 cup diagonally cut snow peas

1 tablespoon fresh ginger, peeled &grated

1/2 cup onion, vertically sliced

2 cups cooked long-grain white rice

1/4 cup of green onions, sliced

1/4 cup of roasted peanuts, unsalted& chopped

1/4 teaspoon salt

<u>Direction</u>

1. In a small bowl, mix together 2 teaspoons of sesame oil, chicken broth, soy sauce, vinegar, chicken paste, cornstarch and salt.

2. Set wok on medium-high temperature. Add the 1 teaspoon of sesame oil that is left and 1 tablespoon of canola oil and then swirl.

3. Now add the chicken; stir-fry for 2 minutes and remove from wok.

4. Add the remaining 1 tablespoon of canola oil and swirl. Add the bell peppers, snow peas, onions, ginger and garlic and stir-fry for 1 minute.

5. Add the broth mixture; cook until thick. Return the chicken to wok and cook until chicken is done.

6. Ladle 1/2 cup of rice onto 1 plate out of 4 and top with 1 cup of chicken mixture, peanuts and green onions. Repeat with the remaining 3 plates.

Classic Chicken Chow Mein
Serves: 2

<u>Ingredients</u>

11 oz skinless chicken breasts, cut into strips

1 tablespoon of cornstarch

1 teaspoon five-spice powder

1 large spring onion (green), sliced lengthwise

2 tablespoons light soy sauce

1 teaspoon of sesame oil or as needed

5 oz bean sprouts

2 tablespoons groundnut oil (peanut)

1 teaspoon chile sauce, optional

1 red bell pepper, seeded & finely sliced

 Dash of dark soy sauce

Freshly ground black pepper, finely ground

5 oz medium egg noodles or dried yellow Shi wheat flour noodles (found at specialty Asian markets)

Directions

1. In a pan of boiling water, cook the noodles until al dente or instructed in the package.

2. Drain, run under cold running water and then re-drain. Drizzle with sesame oil, and toss through so it doesn't stick.

3. Season the chicken with chili sauce, if using, a splash of dark soy sauce and five-spice powder. Mix thoroughly. Lightly coat the chicken breasts with the cornstarch.

4. Place a wok on high heat, add the peanut or groundnut oil and heat until smoking. Add the chicken, stir-frying until cooked through.

5. Add the red bell pepper, stir-frying1 minute, then add the green onion and bean sprouts and stir-fry 30-45 seconds.

6. Now add the cooked noodles, season with black pepper, light soy sauce and 1 teaspoon of toasted sesame oil.

7. Stir and serve immediately.

Asian-Style Sweet & Hot Pepper Chicken

Serves: 4- 6

<u>Ingredients</u>

1 1/2 pounds chicken breast, boneless, skinless& diced into 1-inch cubes

1/2 cup ketchup

1 tablespoon of soy sauce

2 teaspoons green onion bottoms, minced

1 1/2 teaspoons cornstarch

1/4 cup chicken stock

1 1/2 teaspoons dark soy sauce

1 tablespoon chili garlic sauce

2 teaspoons sugar

2 teaspoons minced ginger

4 teaspoons vegetable oil

2 teaspoons minced garlic

1 jalapeno, stemmed, seeded& thinly sliced

10 dried red chiles

1 red bell pepper, stemmed, seeded &thinly sliced

2 teaspoons toasted sesame seeds

1 cup yellow onion, sliced

1 tablespoon fresh cilantro leaves, chopped

1 teaspoon of sesame oil

<u>Directions</u>

1. Combine the dark soy, soy sauce and cornstarch in a medium bowl. Whisk to blend and then add the chicken to it. Toss to coat the chicken evenly; set aside 15 to 20 minutes.

2. Combine the chili garlic sauce, ketchup and sugar in a medium bowl. Stir and set aside.

3. Place a wok over high heat; add the vegetable oil to it and swirl to ensure wok is well coated with the oil.

4. Now add the garlic, ginger, green onions, jalapenos and dried chilies to the wok. Cook and stir at least 20 seconds until the chilies begin to brown and the garlic is fragrant.

5. Add the onions, chicken and bell peppers and stir-fry 5 minutes or until the chicken loses its pinkness.

6. Add the sauce to the wok and bring to a boil, tossing well to coat the chicken and veggies evenly.

7. Add the sesame seeds, cilantro and sesame oil and toss to combine well. Remove and serve with steamed white rice.

The General's Chicken

Serves: 6

<u>Ingredients</u>

Meat:

3 lbs deboned dark chicken meat, cut into large chunks

16 small dried hot peppers

1 tsp white pepper

1 cup cornstarch

1 egg

1/4 cup of soy sauce

Vegetable oil for deep-frying

Sauce:

1+1/2 cup hot chicken broth

1/2 cup cornstarch

1+1/2 tsp minced garlic

1/4 cup white vinegar

1+1/2 tsp minced ginger root

1/2 cup soy sauce

3/4 cup sugar

1/4 cup cooking wine

1 tsp monosodium glutamate (optional)

1/4 cup water

<u>Directions</u>

1. Combine 1/2 cup of cornstarch and water. Add sugar, garlic, vinegar, ginger, chicken broth 1/2 cup of soy sauce, wine and MSG if using. Stir until the sugar dissolves and place in the refrigerator until needed.

2. In a separate bowl, combine chicken, white pepper, egg and1/4 cup soy sauce, stirring well.

3. Add 1 cup of cornstarch and mix again until chicken pieces are evenly coated. Add a cup of vegetable oil to assist in separating the chicken pieces.

4. Divide the chicken into small quantities. Deep-fry until crispy and then drain on paper towels.

5. Add a little amount of oil to the wok and heat until the wok is hot. Add pepper and onions and stir-fry a little. Stir the sauce and add it to the wok.

6. Place the chicken in the sauce and cook until the sauce thickens.

Chicken Kung Po

Serves: 2 to 4

<u>Ingredients</u>

Chicken:

2 skinless chicken breasts or 4 chicken thighs, cut into 1/2-inch slices

1 tablespoon peanut oil

Handful of dry-roasted cashews

1 tablespoon of cornstarch or potato flour

4 dried red chiles

2 tablespoons Sichuan peppercorns

2 scallions, chopped into 1-inch lengths

1 tablespoon dry sherry or Shaohsing rice wine

Salt and ground white pepper

1 red bell pepper, seeded & cut into chunks

Sauce:

1 tablespoon of cornstarch

7 tablespoons cold vegetable stock

1 tablespoon hoisin sauce

1 tablespoon light soy sauce

1 tablespoon ketchup

1 tablespoon balsamic vinegar or Chinkiang black rice vinegar

1 teaspoon chili sauce

<u>Directions</u>

1. For the chicken: Place the chicken pieces in a bowl and season with salt and pepper. Add the cornstarch or potato flour and mix thoroughly to coat the chicken pieces.

2. For the sauce: Combine the cornstarch, vegetable stock, soy sauce, hoisin sauce, ketchup, chili sauce and vinegar to a medium bowl and stir well.

3. Heat the wok over high heat until it begins to smoke. Add the peanut oil, the dried chiles and Sichuan peppercorns and fry for about 15 seconds.

4. Now add the chicken pieces and stir-fry at least 2 minutes. Once the chicken starts to turn opaque, add the dry sherry or rice wine. Cook for 2 minutes and then add the sauce.

5. Bring the mixture to a boil and then add the red pepper, cooking another 2 minutes until the meat is fully cooked and the sauce thickens with a sticky consistently.

6. Finally add the scallions, cook for 1 minute and then add the cashews. Transfer to a platter and serve.

Spicy Nuoc Mam Chicken

Enjoy this deliciously hot dish with Broccoli.

Serves: 3 to 4

Ingredients

1½ pounds boneless, skinless chicken breast, thinly sliced crosswise

1 tablespoon (6 g) grated ginger

2- 3 tablespoons peanut oil

2 cloves garlic, crushed or 1 teaspoon minced garlic

2 tablespoons Splenda

1 teaspoon fish sauce (nuoc mam)

¼ cup soy sauce

¾ cup dry white wine

2 - 3 little red chilies, finely minced or 1 fresh jalapeño

Guar or xanthan

1 teaspoon pepper

Directions

1. Place a wok over high heat. Add the oil and heat for 1-2 minutes. Add the ginger and garlic, stirring to flavor the oil for at least 1 minute.

2. Add the chicken, stir-fry for 1- 2 minutes and then add the soy sauce, splenda, fish sauce, jalapeño, white wine and pepper, stirring frequently until chicken is cooked through.

3. Thicken the pan juices slightly with xanthan or guar and then serve.

Moo Goo Gai Wok

Serves 4:6

<u>Ingredients</u>

4 chicken breast halves, skinned, boned& sliced

4 lb. bok choy, chopped

8 oz. fresh mushrooms, sliced

6 scallions, chopped

5 tablespoons corn oil

4 cloves garlic, minced

1 tablespoon of cornstarch

4 tablespoons soy sauce

2 tablespoons sugar

2 cups water

Salt and pepper

<u>Directions</u>

1. Mix the pepper, salt, cornstarch and garlic together in a bowl. Add the chicken and season with salt and pepper. Set aside.

2. Add 3 tablespoons of corn oil to a wok, let it heat and then stir in bok choy, sugar and mushrooms for 2 minutes. Cover and cook 5 minutes and then remove from wok.

3. Heat the remaining 2 tablespoons of corn oil in the wok. Stir-fry over high heat for 2 minutes. Add soy sauce, mixing well.

4. Cover and cook until the chicken is well cooked. Now mix in the scallions and cooked vegetables.

5. Stir fry at least 1 minute and serve hot with rice.

Chicken &Veggies Stir-Fry
Serves: 4

<u>Ingredients</u>

6 oz Chinese pea pods (fresh) or1 package Chinese pea pods (frozen)

1 teaspoon soy sauce

1 pound boneless, skinless chicken breast, cut into strips

1 teaspoon cornstarch

1 egg white

1 teaspoon finely chopped gingerroot

3 cups celery, sliced on the bias

2 cloves garlic, finely chopped

1 teaspoon soy sauce

1 can (8 ounces) water chestnuts, sliced& drained

2 cups sliced mushrooms

2 tablespoons cornstarch

1 can (8 ounces) bamboo shoots, sliced& drained

¾ cup chicken broth

½ teaspoon sugar

1 tablespoon vegetable oil

1 tablespoon vegetable oil

¼ cup cold water

Directions

1. Combine chicken, 1 teaspoon of soy sauce, 1 teaspoon of cornstarch and egg white in a bowl. Cover and chill for 30 minutes.

2. Meanwhile, rinse the frozen pea pods with cold water to separate or remove the strings from the fresh pea pods; drain.

3. Heat 1 tablespoon of oil in a wok until hot. Add gingerroot and garlic, stir-frying over medium heat until light brown.

4. Add celery and pea pods; stir-fry for 1 minute. Add water chestnuts, bamboo shoots and mushrooms, stir-fry another 1 minute. Remove the vegetables with a slotted spoon.

5. Heat 1 tablespoon of oil in the wok until hot. Add the chicken; stir-fry it over high heat until white.

6. Stir in the sugar and broth. Heat to boiling and then reduce heat. Cover and let it simmer for 2 minutes, stirring infrequently.

7. Mix 2tablespoons of cornstarch, 1 teaspoon of soy sauce and cold water in a bowl. Stir this mixture into the chicken mixture. Heat to boiling, stirring constantly.

8. Boil and stir for 1 minute. Add vegetables; cook and stir until hot. Serve and enjoy!

Thai Chicken Basil Stir-Fry

Try this Thai-chicken stir fry; it is an interesting change from the usual Chinese stir-fries.

Serves: 3

Ingredients

3 skinless, boneless, chicken breasts cut into ½-inch cubes

2 tablespoons Thai fish sauce

1 teaspoon Splenda

2 cloves garlic, crushed

2 tablespoons soy sauce

¼ teaspoon guar or xanthan

2 teaspoons dried basil

1½ teaspoons of red pepper flakes

Peanut, canola, or coconut oil

1½ cups frozen, crosscut green beans, thawed

1 small onion, sliced

Directions

1. Combine the, soy sauce, fish sauce, Splenda, xanthan or guar in a blender. Blend about 20 seconds and then turn off the blender.

2 Add the red pepper flakes and basil. Set aside.

3. Heat a few tablespoons of oil in a wok over high heat. Once hot, add the chicken, onion and garlic, stir-frying for 3 to 4 minutes.

4. Add the green beans and keep stir-frying until the chicken is thoroughly cooked.

5. Add the fish sauce mixture to the stir-fry and stir. Reduce heat to medium, cover, and simmer for 2- 3 minutes until the beans is tender-crisp.

Chicken& Creamed Corn Soup
Serves: 4-6

Ingredients

1¼ cup cooked and shredded chicken

1 tablespoon peanut oil

2 cups creamed corn

1 clove garlic, crushed

4 cups chicken stock

1 teaspoon ground black pepper

1 tablespoon of finely chopped parsley

4 egg whites

4 green onions, sliced

Directions

1. Place Wok on high heat. Add the oil, garlic, corn, and chicken pieces into the wok and stir-fry 1 minute.

2. Next, add the chicken stock and bring to a boil, reduce heat and add the egg whites, stirring to break them up.

4. Season with parsley and pepper. Enjoy with sliced green onions.

Chinese Garlic Chicken

Serves: 4

<u>Ingredients:</u>

4 boneless & skinless chicken breast halves

4 green onions, sliced thinly on the diagonal

2 tablespoons vegetable oil

1 egg white

1 tablespoon dry white wine or sherry

1 tablespoon cornstarch

1 teaspoon minced gingerroot, minced

6 medium fresh garlic cloves, minced to 3 teaspoons

Hot cooked rice

<u>Directions:</u>

1. Place the chicken breasts in the freezer for 1or 2 hours; chicken shouldn't be frozen solid but just very firm. Slice them crosswise into thin shreds.

2. Beat egg white lightly in small bowl and then stir in cornstarch and wine until dissolved. Add chicken, mixing well to coat. Let it sit for30 minutes at room temperature.

3. Combine the sauce ingredients and mix well. Heat wok and add oil; stir-fry chicken until the pinkness vanishes.

4. Remove chicken. Add ginger, onions and ginger to the wok and stir-fry until ginger and garlic are fragrant but not brown.

5. Place the chicken back to the wok: stir sauce ingredients again and add to wok.

6. Cook and keep stirring until the mixture is hot and bubbly, thickens a little and fully combined.

7. Turn heat off and sprinkle with 1 teaspoon of dark sesame oil. Serve it over rice.

Chicken Lo Mein
Serves: 4

Ingredients

4 cups cooked Chinese noodles, rinsed & drained

12 oz. diced cooked chicken

1 package French−style green beans, frozen & thawed

1 slice ginger, shredded

2 cups fresh bean sprouts

3 scallions, chopped

2 tablespoon sherry

1 teaspoon MSG

1 clove garlic, minced

1 teaspoon sugar

3/4 cup vegetable oil

1/4 teaspoon sesame oil

1/4 cup soy sauce

Directions

1. Combine MSG, soy sauce and sugar in a bowl and set aside. Heat the wok hot and dry.

2. Add all the sesame oil and 3 tablespoons of the vegetable oil. Add ginger and garlic to brown then add all the other vegetables. Stir and cook 1minute over high heat.

3. Now add the sherry. Cover, cook for 1 more minute. Turn heat off. Remove the vegetables, drain, discard juices and set aside the drained vegetables.

4. Heat wok dry again. Add the remaining oil. Turn the heat to medium. Add the cooked noodles and stir often for about 3-4 minutes.

5. Add the chicken and the reserved vegetables; mix well. Stir in the reserved soy sauce mixture, stirring until the noodles become one even color. Enjoy!

BEEF RECIPES

Japanese Teriyaki Beef
Serves: 4-6

Ingredients

2 tablespoons peanut oil

1¾lb beef strips (750g)

¼ cup soy sauce (60ml)

2 tablespoons mirin

2 teaspoons sake (10ml)

2 teaspoons granulated sugar

1 zucchini, cut into batons

1 carrot, finely sliced

5 oz spinach leaves

Directions

1. Place beef strips in a bowl, add the mirin, soy, sugar and sake and marinate 4 hours.

2. Place wok on high heat, add the peanut oil. Sear 1/3 of the beef strips quickly, to seal in the juices and then remove. Repeat process for all beef strips.

3. Add the zucchini and carrot, cook 2 minutes, add the beef and spinach and stir-fry until the spinach has wilted.

Serve immediately with steamed new potatoes.

Beef &Green Pepper Stir-Fry
Serves: 2-4

Ingredients

1/2 lb. flank or skirt steak, cut into thin strips

1 small green bell pepper, sliced thinly

2 1/2 tbsp. soy sauce

1 tablespoon of oriental sesame oil

1 tbsp. dry white wine

3 tsp. cornstarch

1 garlic clove, minced

1 teaspoon of minced peeled fresh ginger

1/4 c. canned beef broth

1 (8 oz.) can sliced water chestnuts, drained

6 tbsp. vegetable oil

Rice, freshly cooked

Directions

1. In a medium bowl, add together 1 ½ tablespoons of soy sauce, sesame oil, wine, 2 teaspoons of cornstarch, garlic and ginger.

2, Add beef, stir to coat and set aside for 30 minutes. In a small bowl, add together broth, the 1 tablespoon of soy sauce that is left as well as the remaining 1 teaspoon of cornstarch.

3. Heat 3 tablespoons of vegetable oil in a wok over high heat. Add the bell pepper and water chestnuts and stir-fry for 2 minutes. Remove from wok.

4. Heat the rest of the 3 tablespoons of oil in the wok, add beef with the marinade and stir fry about 4 minutes.

5. Return pepper and water chestnuts to wok and mix thoroughly.

6. Stir the broth mixture and add to wok. Cook about 30 seconds or until sauce thickens. Serve with rice.

Oriental Peppered Steak
Serves: 4

Ingredients

1 pound round steak, sliced thinly into strips

1 cup beef broth

1 tablespoon cornstarch

1 tablespoon of soy sauce

1 tablespoon oil

2 small onions, peeled & each cut into 6 wedges

1 clove garlic, peeled & minced

2 green peppers, cored, seeded & cut into thin strips of 1½ inch long

2 tomatoes, each cut into 8 wedges

¼ teaspoon freshly ground black pepper

½ teaspoon fresh gingerroot, peeled & minced

Directions

1. Combine the cornstarch, beef and soy sauce and set aside.

2. Heat the oil in a wok and add garlic and meat, stir-frying until done.

3. Add tomatoes onion and peppers and stir-fry for 1 or 2 minutes. Add ginger and pepper.

4. Stir the cornstarch mixture and add to wok; stir-fry until sauce thickens a little. Serve immediately.

Asian Beef Stir-Fry

Serves: 3

Ingredients

1 lb lean steak

6 oz dry wheat spaghetti

3 cloves garlic, minced

1/8 tsp crushed red pepper flakes

1 onion, sliced

1 head napa cabbage, shredded

4 celery stalks, sliced

1/2 cup lite soy sauce

Directions

1. Prepare spaghetti as directed; drain and set aside.

2. Meanwhile, cut steak into 2 inch strips lengthwise. Cut again crosswise into slices of 1/8 inch thick.

3. Lightly coat a wok with cooking spray, stir-fry garlic and red pepper flakes over medium-high heat for a minute.

4. Add the steak strips to wok, stir-fry just about 2 minutes to remove pink color. Remove steak and set aside.

5. Recoat the wok lightly with cooking spray. Stir-fry celery and onion until tender, add cabbage and cook until crispy tender.

6. Return steak to wok. Add lite soy sauce and cooked spaghetti and mix gently, heating thoroughly. Serve and enjoy.

Thai-ish Basil Beef Stir-Fry

Serves: 3

Ingredients

1 pound boneless chuck, thinly sliced across grain

½ cup peanut oil or other bland oil

6 scallions, crisp green part included, cut into 1-inch lengths

2 teaspoons basil, dried or 2 tablespoons fresh basil, chopped

¼ teaspoon Splenda

1 tablespoon of soy sauce

Pepper

Direction

1. Heat the oil in a wok over high heat. Add the beef and stir-fry 1-2 minutes.

2. Add the basil, Splenda, soy sauce and season with pepper. Add the scallions and stir-fry 3-4 minutes.

3. Toss with the beef and cook 1-2 minutes. Serve.

Changsha Beef

Serves: 4

Ingredients

2 tablespoons cooking oil

2 cups of broccoli florets

2 teaspoons minced garlic

1 teaspoon cornstarch dissolved in 2 teaspoons water

4 small dried red chilies

Marinade:

2 teaspoons cornstarch

2 tablespoons soy sauce

3/4 pound flank steak, sliced thinly across the grain

1 tablespoon dry sherry

Sauce:

1 tablespoon of soy sauce

1 tablespoon Chinese rice wine

2 teaspoons sugar

3 tablespoons Chinese black vinegar or balsamic vinegar

1 teaspoon of sesame oil

2 teaspoons chili garlic sauce

Direction

1. Add together, in a bowl, all the marinade ingredients. Add beef and stir. Let it stand 10 minutes.

2. Combine all the sauce ingredients in a bowl.

3. In a large pot, pour 1 inch water and bring to a boil. Place the broccoli in it and boil 2 to 3 minutes (let it be tender-crisp) then drain.

4. Heat a wok over high heat. Once hot, add oil and swirl to coat sides. Add chilies and garlic about 10 seconds until fragrant. Add beef and stir-fry for 1½ to 2 minutes.

5. Add the broccoli and sauce and bring to a boil. Add the cornstarch solution. Cook and stir, until the sauce thickens.

Burger Chop Suey

Serves: 4

<u>Ingredients</u>

1 pound ground round

1 medium onion, sliced

2 cups mushrooms, sliced

2 stalks celery, thinly sliced diagonally

½ teaspoon minced garlic or 1 clove garlic, crushed

½ green pepper, diced

2 cups bean sprouts

 1/3 soy sauce

½ teaspoon liquid beef bouillon conce ntrate

2 tablespoons oil

<u>Directions</u>

1. In a wok over high heat, brown the beef in oil and break it up. When it's almost browned, add garlic, onion, green pepper, mushrooms and celery.

2. Keep breaking the meat up while stir-frying the veggies. When the pink color is gone from the beef and the veggies are just tender-crisp, add the soy sauce beef bouillon concentrate and bean sprouts.

3. Keep stir-frying until the bean sprouts are on the verge of wilting then serve.

Border South Stir-Fry

Serves: 4

<u>Ingredients</u>

1 can (7 ounces) whole kernel corn with sweet peppers

1 pound beef top round steak, partially frozen

2 tablespoons snipped parsley

2 teaspoons vinegar

½ teaspoon sugar

½ teaspoon ground cumin

¾ teaspoon cornstarch

1 cup salsa

1/8 teaspoon ground cinnamon

¼ teaspoon pepper

1 teaspoon oil

1 small onion, chopped

1 clove garlic, minced

½ cup shredded Monterey Jack cheese

Tomatoes (optional)

Chili peppers (optional)

Tortilla chips (optional)

¼ cup water

Shredded lettuce

Direction

1. Cut partially frozen beef on the bias into thin strips.

2. For the sauce add together ½ cup of salsa, parsley, water, cornstarch, vinegar, cinnamon, pepper sugar and cumin to a small bowl, stir and set aside.

3. Preheat wok over high heat and add the oil. Stir-fry garlic in the heated oil for 15 seconds. Add onion, stir-fry until tender and then remove onion.

4. Add half of the beef. Stir-fry until done. Remove and stir-fry the rest of the beef for until done. Return all the beef to wok. Push beef from the center of wok.

5. Stir sauce and add to center of wok. Cook and stir until thickened. Cook and stir for another 2 minutes.

6. Return onion to wok; add corn. Stir together ingredients to coat with sauce, cover wok and cook 1 minute.

7. Place lettuce on each of the 4 plates and top with meat mixture, the remaining salsa and cheese. If desired, garnish with hot peppers, tomatoes and tortilla chips.

Woked Beef With Hoisin Sauce

Serves: 2

Ingredients

200g lean sirloin steaks, sliced thinly across the grain

1 tsp finely fresh root ginger, chopped or jar- fresh ginger paste

1 tbsp dry sherry

1 tbsp soy sauce

2 tsp sesame oil

1 fat garlic clove, crushed

3 tbsp hoisin sauce

1 tbsp sunflower oil

1 tbsp sesame seeds

1 large carrot, cut into matchsticks

140g mushrooms, sliced

100g mangetout, halved lengthways

Chinese noodles, to serve

Directions

1. Combine soy sauce, sesame oil, sherry, ginger and garlic in a shallow dish. Add steak and marinate for about 30 minutes.

2. Add the sesame seeds to a heated wok and toast over high heat, stirring until golden. Remove to plate.

3. Heat the sunflower oil in a wok until hot. Now add the steak, including the marinade, and stir fry over a high heat until lightly browned. Remove to a plate but leave the juices in the wok.

4. Add the carrots to wok and stir fry for 3-5 minutes add the mangetout and cook another 2 minutes.

5. Return steak to wok, add the mushrooms and toss all together. Finally, add the hoisin sauce and stir fry 1 minute.

6. Sprinkle with the toasted sesame seeds.

Orange Ginger Beef Stir-fry
Serves: 4

Ingredients

1 orange

½ cup hoisin sauce

½ tsp Chinese Five Spice

¼ tsp dried chili pepper flakes

1 lb Beef Top Sirloin Grilling Steak, ¾-inch thick

1 tbsp cornstarch& minced ginger root each

2 tsp vegetable oil

4 cup cut stir-fry vegetables

2 cloves garlic, minced

Directions

1. Grate orange peel thinly and squeeze out juice.

2. Combine ginger root, hoisin sauce, cornstarch, orange juice, 1/4 tsp of the orange peel, pepper flakes and Chinese Five Spice; set aside.

3. Cut steak into two lengthwise. Cut crosswise into 1/4-inch strips and remove all fat.

4. Heat oil in wok until sizzling and then stir-fry garlic and beef until beef is browned but pinkish inside (stir-fry in 2 batches). Remove beef.

5. Add veggies and 4-6 spoonfuls of water to wok; cover and cook until tender-crisp.

6. Now add the reserved sauce; cooking and stirring until thickened. Add beef and any juices; stir and heat through.

Woked Beef Stroganoff

Serves: 4

<u>Ingredients</u>

1 1/2 lb. boneless beef

5 tbsp. butter

Pepper

1 med. onion, chopped

3 tbsp. flour

1/2 lb. mushrooms

1 cup beef bouillon

1/4 tsp. nutmeg

1 tbsp. Dijon mustard

Hot, cooked buttered noodles

1/2 cup whipping cream

<u>Directions</u>

1. Cut the beef in strips of 1/4 inch and sprinkle with pepper.

2. Add butter in wok and once it melts, stir-fry onion until limp. Now add ½ of the meat and cook. Remove and add the second half.

3. Remove the meat and add butter to the wok. Add the mushrooms and stir until limp.

4. Add the flour and cook 30 seconds. Lower heat, add mustard and broth, stir until thickened.

5. Return the meat/onion mixture. Add cream and nutmeg, stir together and serve over noodles.

Thai Beef And Spinach Stir -Fry
Serves: 4

Ingredients

5 oz baby spinach (150g)

2 brown onions, sliced

¾ cup peanut oil, divided

1 tablespoon finely diced ginger

1 teaspoon lemon grass, thinly sliced

2 cloves garlic, finely sliced

2 red bell peppers, cut in strips

1¾lbslean beef strips (750g)

½ cup roasted cashews (60g)

4 tablespoons of mint leaves

2 teaspoons fish sauce

1 tablespoon lime juice

2 tablespoons sweet Thai chili sauce

Directions

1. Heat wok over high heat, add 1 tablespoon oil and stir-fry ginger, onions and garlic. Cook 2 minutes.

2. Add the bell peppers, cook another 2 minutes and remove.

2. Add remaining oil that's left and stir-fry the beef1 - 2 minutes in small batches.

3. Return all ingredients to wok, lower heat and cook until spinach has softened.

Enjoy with coconut rice.

Beef With Snow Peas
Serves: 6

Ingredients

2 lb. beef steak, thinly sliced

2 pkg. frozen snow peas (thawed & drained)

1/4 cup oil

1 lg. onion, chopped

1 tsp. sugar

1 tbsp. soy sauce

Spicy Marinade:

1 tbsp. soy sauce

2 tbsp. oil

1 clove garlic, minced

1 tbsp. catsup

1 tbsp. cornstarch

1 tbsp. dry sherry

1 tsp. Worcestershire sauce

Directions

1. Combine all the butter ingredients, add beef, cover and chill 6- 9 hours.

2. Add 2 tablespoons of oil to a heated wok. Add onions and peas. Cook until almost tender.

3. Stir in sugar and soy sauce; cook 1 minute. Remove from wok.

4. Add oil and cook beef for 3 minutes. Add marinade sauce and vegetables until beef is done. Serve with noodles or rice.

Beef With Baby Carrots And Sugar Snap Peas
Serves: 1

Ingredients

3 ounces beef flank steak, sliced into 2" pieces

2 tablespoons snow peas or sugar snap

1/2 teaspoon lite soy sauce

1/4 teaspoon fresh ginger, grated

1/8 teaspoon red chili paste

1/2 clove garlic, minced

2 teaspoons water or dry sherry

1/4 teaspoon peanut oil

3 baby carrots, cut into quarters

2 tablespoons low-sodium beef broth

1 teaspoon water

1/2 teaspoon cornstarch

Directions

1. Combine the soy sauce, ginger, chili paste, sherry and garlic and pour over the meat. Marinate 10 minutes to 1 hour.

2. Heat water in a medium pot and bring to a boil. Add the carrots and boil for just about 2 minutes and remove.

3. Add the peas, parboil 1 minute, drain, refresh with cold water and set aside. Remove beef from marinade, drain beef and discard the marinade.

4. Heat a wok over high heat, add the peanut oil and stir-fry beef, about 2 minutes or until just cooked. Add the carrots and peas to wok and toss rapidly in the hot wok.

5. Add the beef broth to the veggies and meat and simmer 3 minutes.

6. Combine the cornstarch and water, mixing until smooth. Add cornstarch solution to beef mixture and simmer 3 minutes.

7. Cook about 2 minutes until the sauce thickens.

Shredded Beef Sautéed

Serves: 4

Ingredients

400 g beef cut into thin strips

1 tbsp brown sugar

5 tbsp soy sauce

½ tbsp black pepper

Bunch of thyme

Bunch of cherry tomatoes

2 tbsp olive oil

2 tbsp five-spice powder

1 tsp sugar

Directions

1. Pre-heat oven to 150°C. Combine five-spice powder, soy sauce, black pepper and brown sugar and coat beef. Let it marinate 30 minutes.

2. Place the thyme, sugar, olive oil and cherry tomatoes in an oven-proof bowl. Place bowl in oven for 45 minutes.

3 Heat the wok over high heat, add 1 tbsp olive oil, fry the beef strips on every side for 1 minute.

4. Serve with rice and tomatoes from the oven.

Mongolian Lamb

Serves: 4-6

Ingredients

1¾lbs lamb, cut into strips (750g)

2 tablespoons rice wine, divided

1 tablespoon light soy sauce

½ teaspoon salt

1 teaspoon sugar

1 tablespoon sesame oil

1 tablespoon of soy sauce

2 tablespoons peanut oil

1 brown onion, diced

2 cloves garlic, diced

1 red pepper, sliced

½ bunch green onions, cut into ¾ inch piece

Directions

1. Place lamb into a bowl; mix with1 tablespoon rice wine and light soy sauce. Let it marinate 30 minutes.

2. Meanwhile, place the regular soy sauce, sugar, 1 tablespoon rice wine, sesame oil, salt and sugar into a tight-fitting jar and shake well

3. Heat the Wok over high heat and add the peanut oil. Once oil is hot, add the vegetables and stir-fry 2 minutes, then remove.

4. Add the meat to Wok and cook 2 minutes. Add the sauce, bring mixture to a boil and return the veggies to heat through.

Serve with steamed rice.

PORK RECIPES

Pineapple Pork

Serves: 2 or 3

<u>Ingredients</u>

12 oz boneless pork loin, cut into thin strips

3 tablespoons rice or cider vinegar

1½ tablespoons of Splenda

½ medium onion, sliced

1 teaspoon soy sauce

3 tablespoons canned, crushed pineapple in juice

¼ teaspoon blackstrap molasses

3 tablespoons oil

½ teaspoon minced garlic

½ medium green pepper, cut into squares

Guar or xanthan

Directions

1. Combine the vinegar, pineapple, splenda, soy sauce, garlic and molasses and set aside.

2. Heat the oil in a wok over high heat.

3. Add the pork, stir-fry until half-done and then add the onions and peppers and stir-fry often.

4. When the pork loses all its pinkness, stir in the vinegar mixture. Simmer 2-3 minutes, stirring until the veggies are tender-crisp.

5. Thicken the pan juices with xanthan or guar and serve.

Sesame Ginger Pork
Serves: 2

Ingredients

12 ounces boneless pork top loin, thinly sliced

2 tablespoons grated ginger

1 teaspoon Splenda

4 teaspoons soy sauce

2 teaspoons toasted sesame oil

4 scallions, sliced, crisp green part included

2 cloves garlic, crushed

2 tablespoons dry sherry

2 tablespoons peanut oil

<u>Directions</u>

1. Combine all ingredients except the pork in a medium-size bowl. Now add the pork, stir well. and marinate for 30 minutes.

2. Heat the wok over high heat; add the pork, marinade inclusive, and stir-fry about 5 minutes.

3. Serve and enjoy!

Pork& Veg Stir-Fry With Cashew Rice
Serves: 4

<u>Ingredients</u>

3/4 cup uncooked long-grain rice

1/3 cup green onions, chopped

1/4 cup dry-roasted cashews, salted& coarsely chopped

2/3 cup fat-free, less-sodium chicken broth

3 tablespoons low-sodium soy sauce, divided

2 tablespoons cornstarch, divided

2 tablespoons honey

1 pork tenderloin (1-pound), trimmed &cut into 1/2-inch cubes

1 tablespoon canola oil, divided

2 cups (about 4 ounces) mushrooms, sliced

1 cup onion, chopped

1 tablespoon fresh ginger, grated& peeled

2 garlic cloves, minced

2 cups (about 6 ounces) sugar snap peas, trimmed

1(1 cup) chopped red bell pepper

1/2 teaspoon salt

Directions

1. Cook the rice as instructed in the package; omit the salt and fat. Add 1/3 cup green onions, dry-roasted cashews, and salt and set aside.

2. In a small bowl, add together 2/3 cup chicken broth, 1 tablespoon cornstarch, honey and 2 tablespoons low-sodium soy sauce; set aside.

3. Add together the remaining 1 tablespoon cornstarch, the remaining 1 tablespoon of soy sauce and the pork in a bowl, tossing well to coat.

4. In a wok, heat 2 teaspoons of oil over medium-high heat. Add pork and sauté until browned. Remove from wok.

5. Add the remaining 1 teaspoon of oil to wok. Add 1 cup of onion and mushrooms; sautéing 2 minutes. Add ginger and garlic; stir and sauté for 30 seconds.

6. Add bell pepper and peas and wok; sauté for a minute. Add pork; stir and sauté for another minute.

7. Now add the reserved broth mixture to the wok and bring to a boil; cook until thick, stirring often. Serve over cashew rice.

Pork Fried Rice And Plantains

Serves: 2 to 3

Ingredients

1 large ripe plantain (partly black)

1/2 pound pork loin

1 large garlic clove

1 medium onion

4 medium scallions

2 teaspoons minced ginger

About 1/2 teaspoon Asian (dark) sesame oil

2 1/2 tablespoons vegetable oil

About 2 tablespoons chopped cilantro

About 3 cups cold, long-grain white rice, cooked

About 2 tablespoons soy sauce

Directions

1. Trim the plantain tips and cut into 2- to 3-inch lengths. On each piece, slit the skin lengthwise, then remove (pull slightly crosswise and not down the length of the piece).

2. Now cut into 1/2-inch slices and then cut into dice of about 1/2-inch. Cut the pork into pieces of the same size. Halve onion then cut into slices, lengthwise. Mince garlic and thinly slice scallions.

3. Heat wok over high flame. Add 1 tablespoon of oil and pork; stir-fry about 2 minutes until browned. Add the plantain; brown per side without stirring. Toss and cook until browned on all sides, Transfer to a plate; reserve.

4. Return wok to heat, add garlic, ginger and1/2 tablespoon oil; stir-fry few seconds. Add onion and cook for 1 minute. Add the remaining tablespoon of oil. Add rice and toss for 1 minute.

5. Add pork and plantain and toss. Add 2 tablespoons cilantro and scallions. Sprinkle with 2 tablespoons of soy sauce and sesame oil and toss again.

6. Taste for seasoning and add cilantro, sesame oil and soy as desired. Ladle onto a platter; serve hot.

Pork BBQ And Fried Rice

Serves: 4 to 6

<u>Ingredients</u>

For The Pork:

1/4 cup oyster sauce

1/4 cup soy sauce

1 tablespoon minced fresh ginger

1 tablespoon sesame oil

1 tablespoon minced garlic

1/4 cup sweet and sour sauce

1 pound pork tenderloin

For The Rice:

1 tablespoon minced fresh ginger

4 tablespoons canola oil

1/2 cup diced red bell pepper

1 cup diced red onion

1/2 cup diced yellow bell pepper

1/2 cup thinly sliced green cabbage

1/2 cup peeled, diced carrot

1/2 cup thinly sliced snap peas

1/2 cup diced celery

6 cups short-grain white rice, cooked & cooled

1 tablespoon minced garlic

3 eggs, beaten

1/4 cup oyster sauce

1/4 cup soy sauce

1 tablespoon sesame oil

2 tablespoons toasted sesame seeds

1/2 cup chopped green onion

Directions

1. For the pork: add soy, oyster sauce, garlic, sesame oil and ginger in medium bowl. Add the pork and place in the refrigerator for 1 hour to marinate.

2. Heat the grill to medium-high, and then grill pork on both sides until done. Heat the marinade that is left to 165 degrees F and use it to baste the meat as it cooks.

3. Once the meat is almost cooked through, glaze the sides with the sweet and sour sauce and let it cook through while sauce caramelizes on the meat.

4. Remove from grill, let it stand 10 minutes, and cut into 1/2-inch pieces.

5. For the rice: heat oil in a wok on high heat until the oil is very hot. Add ginger and all the vegetables but do not add garlic. Cook until veggies are cooked and then add garlic.

6. Before the garlic browns, add the rice quickly and mix immediately to prevent the rice from sticking to the sides of the wok.

7. Once the entire mixture is well combined, pour the beaten eggs over the veggies and rice, tossing rapidly until eggs are all cooked.

8. Add the oyster sauce, soy sauce and sesame oil. Mix well and add pork.

9. Garnish with sesame seeds and green onions. Serve immediately.

Flavored Pork And Cabbage
Yield: 3 servings

So much flavor, so little work…

<u>Ingredients</u>

Canola or peanut oil

1 pound boneless pork loin, thinly sliced

1 small onion, thinly sliced

½ head cabbage, sliced ½ inch thick

1 to 2 tablespoons chili garlic paste

1 tablespoon black bean sauce

<u>Directions</u>

1. In a wok, heat 3 to 4 tablespoons of oil over high heat. Once hot, add the pork and stir-fry for 3- 5 minutes.

2. Add the onion and cabbage and keep stir-frying until the onion and cabbage are just tender-crisp.

3. Add the chili garlic paste and the black bean sauce, stir well and then serve.

Curried Pork And Chili Salad
Serves: 4-6

<u>Ingredients</u>

2 tablespoons peanut oil

1 tablespoon Thai green curry paste

½ cup peanuts

2 cloves garlic, lightly crushed

¾lb ground pork (300g)

1 tablespoon brown sugar

2 teaspoons fish sauce (10ml)

2 tomatoes, cut into wedges

1 head iceberg lettuce, washed

<u>Directions</u>

1. Heat wok over high heat until hot and then add the oil, curry paste and nuts, cooking for a few minutes.

2. Add the ground pork, stir to brown and then add the fish sauce and brown sugar; stir-fry until liquid evaporates.

3. Arrange the lettuce on platter, top with tomato and finally the pork mixture.

Pork Sang Chy Bow

(Chinese lettuce rolls)

Serves: 4-6

Ingredients

1 egg yolk

2 cups ground pork (500g)

3 cloves garlic, finely diced

4 oz bamboo shoots, finely sliced (120g)

2 oz water chestnuts, finely diced

4 shitake mushrooms, diced

2 green onions, finely sliced

2 tablespoons vegetable oil

Sauce:

1 head Iceberg lettuce

1 tablespoon of soy sauce (15ml)

1 tablespoon oyster sauce

1 teaspoon of sesame oil (5ml)

Directions

1. Combine the vegetables, ground pork and egg yolk.

2. Heat the wok over high heat, and add the oil, pork and vegetable mixture, stir-frying until pork is cooked.

3. Now add the sauce ingredients and cook 1 minute.

4. Place mixture into prepared lettuce cups. Enjoy!

Pork & Rice Stick Noodles

Serves: 4-6

Ingredients

¼lb rice stick noodles (110g)

2 tablespoons soy sauce (30ml)

1 tablespoon dry sherry

1 teaspoon chili paste

1 teaspoon sugar

½ teaspoon garlic

½ cup beef stock (125ml)

2 tablespoons peanut or vegetable oil (30ml)

½ lb (250g) pork fillet, sliced finely in (1cm) 1/3 inch rounds

1 teaspoon grated ginger

2 green shallots, sliced

1 punnet baby corn sliced in half

½ cup sliced water chestnuts

Directions

1. Place water in a bowl and bring to a boil. Place the noodles in it for 5 minutes to soften.

2. Drain the noodles and cut about 2inch lengths (5cm). Combine the soy sauce, rice sherry, chili paste, garlic, sugar and beef stock in a small bowl.

3. Place the wok on high heat and add the oil, then pork and stir-fry 3 - 4minutes.

4. Add the water chestnuts, ginger and green shallots, cook for another 30 seconds.

5. Add the drained noodles and soy mixture, lower heat and cook until the liquid is almost absorbed but moist still.

6. Taste for seasoning and adjust as desired. Enjoy with steamed Chinese green veggies.

VEGETABLE RECIPES

Hot Scallops With Baby Bok Choy

Serves: 4

<u>Ingredients</u>

12 scallops

1 tin of black beans

2 tablespoon chicken stock

1 teaspoon cornflour

1 tbsp light soy sauce

1 tablespoon ginger, finely chopped

2 tablespoon peanut oil

2 cloves of garlic, finely chopped

1 red pepper, deseeded and cut into strips

4 baby bok choy, cleaned& nicely chopped

1 spring onion, finely chopped

<u>Directions</u>

1. Clean the scallops and pat dry.

2. In a bowl, combine the black beans, stock, soy sauce and cornflour.

3. Heat a wok over high heat; add oil to it, and once hot, add the ginger and garlic. Stir-fry 1 minute.

4 Add the scallops and fry lovely brown in color. Remove scallops from wok.

5. Add together the spring onion, bok choy, black bean mixture and pepper, and fry about a minute.

6. Add the scallops and cook about 1 minute.

Ratatouille Relish
Serves: 8

<u>Ingredients</u>

1½ teaspoons dried oregano

3 cups eggplant, chopped & cut into 1-inch cubes

¾ cup olive oil

1 medium onion, sliced

3 cups zucchini, sliced

3 cloves garlic

2 green peppers, cut into strips

1 can (4 ounces) sliced black olives, drained

1 can (14½ ounces) sliced tomatoes, undrained

½ teaspoon salt

¼ teaspoon pepper

Direction

1. Heat the oil in a wok over medium heat. Add the zucchini, eggplant, peppers, garlic and onion.

2. Sauté 15- 20 minutes, turning occasionally to let the vegetables coat well with the oil.

3. Once the vegetables are about half-cooked, add the tomatoes (liquid inclusive), oregano, olives, salt and pepper.

4. Stir, cover, reduce heat to low, simmer 30- 40 minutes. Serve.

Asian Broccoli With Wine And Sugar

Wine, sugar and ginger combined make a flavor-rich seasoning for healthy and delicious meal.

Serves: 4

Ingredients:

1 teaspoon olive or vegetable oil

1 pound Chinese broccoli

1 tablespoon cooking wine

½ teaspoon minced ginger

½ cup supreme stock (*see table of content*) or chicken broth

1 teaspoon sugar

½ teaspoon salt

<u>Directions</u>

1. Separate broccoli stems from leaves, and cut them into 2-inch sections.

2. Heat a wok over medium- high heat, add oil and swirl to coat sides.

3. Add the stems, sauté a few seconds, add Chinese broccoli leaves, ginger, wine and sugar and keep stir-frying.

4. Add stock, cover wok and cook Chinese broccoli about 1 minute or until tender but crisp with a bright green color.

6. Add salt, mix thoroughly and serve.

Mushrooms/ Tofu Sautéed
Serves: 4 to 6

<u>Ingredients</u>

14 ounces (1 package) firm tofu, drained

Sauce:

1 1/2 tablespoon hoisin sauce

2/3 cup vegetable broth

1/2 teaspoon sesame oil

1 leek (1-inch diameter), white part only, cut into 1/4-inch-thick rounds

1 1/2 teaspoon cornstarch dissolved in 1 tablespoon of water

2 tablespoons cooking oil

1 serrano or jalapeno chili pepper, sliced thinly

1/2 pound portobello mushrooms, sliced into 1-inch squares

1/2 pound small white button mushrooms, halved

6 medium shiitake mushrooms, fresh ones with stems discarded& quartered

Directions

1. Cut the tofu horizontally in half to make two pieces of 3/4-inch thick per piece. Use a 2-inch biscuit cutter to cut 6 rounds from each of the half to make 12 rounds total.

2. Combine1 ½ tablespoon of hoisin sauce, 2/3 cup of vegetable broth and 1/2 teaspoon of sesame oil in a bowl.

3. Place a skillet over medium heat until hot. Now add 1 tablespoon of cooking oil and swirl to coat sides.

4. Add tofu, cook and turn once, about 1 ½ minutes per side until golden brown. Remove skillet from heat.

5. Place a wok over highest heat until hot. Add the 1 tablespoon oil that is left, swirling to coat sides. Now add all mushrooms, leek and chili pepper, stir-frying 1 minute.

6. Add sauce. Turn heat to low, cover and simmer about 5 minutes until mushrooms are tender.

7. Add cornstarch solution. Cook and stir until the sauce boils.

8. Serve by arranging tofu in a circle around the edge of the plate and then place the mushroom mixture in the center.

Happy Fried Noodles & Vegetables

Serves: 5 servings

<u>Ingredients:</u>

1 pound egg noodles

10 cups of water

1 tablespoon olive or vegetable oil, divided

1 cup bamboo shoots, julienned, thinly sliced

3 cups bean sprout

½ cup shredded carrots

2 green onions, julienned

½ cup of shiitake mushrooms, dried, soaked, stems taken out, and julienned

1 teaspoon sugar

½ teaspoon salt

1 tablespoon soy sauce

<u>Directions</u>

1. Pour 10 cups of water in a large pot and bring to boil on high setting. Cook noodles in boiling water 5 - 7 minutes or until al-dente. Drain and set aside.

2. Heat a wok over high heat. Add ½ tablespoon oil, swirl to coat wok, add noodles and pan-fry 7 to 10 minutes or until golden. Remove noodles from wok.

3. Add remaining half tablespoon of oil to wok, add vegetables, stir-fry5 to 7 minutes until just cooked.

4. Return noodles to the wok; add soy sauce, salt and sugar. Stir and serve.

Braised Lotus With Leek Duck

Serves: 4

Ingredients

8 black mushrooms, dried & soaked in for 1 hour warm water then drained, de-stemmed& quartered

1/2 teaspoon Szechwan peppercorns

1 quart chicken stock for steaming

1 (4 to 5 pound) duck, washed, cleaned and patted dry

4 ounces dried lotus seeds, soaked in warm water for 3 hours and drained

5 cups peanut oil

2 leeks, white part julienned & washed thoroughly

6 slices peeled ginger

1/4 pound bacon, 1/8-inch pieces

2 tablespoons salt

1 teaspoon white pepper

Sauce:

1 tablespoon dark soy sauce

1 tablespoon oyster sauce

1 tablespoon shaoxing

1/2 tablespoon ginger julienned

1 tablespoon sugar

2 tablespoons butter

Directions

1. Add the salt and pepper together. Rub the inside and outside of the duck with the salt mix.

2. Add peanut oil to the wok and heat until very hot. Place the duck in the hot oil and spoon the oil for about 5 minutes until duck is golden brown. Drain thoroughly.

3. Combine ginger, lotus, mushrooms, bacon and leeks in a bowl. Stuff the duck with the mix and place on an oval plate and cover.

4. Pour chicken stock into a wok; place a rack in the wok to accommodate the plate. Cover and steam over medium heat for 21/2 hours. Remove plate.

5. Increase the wok to high heat, add the sauce ingredients and add just 1 cup of stock, if necessary.

6. Add the butter, whisking well. Check for seasoning.

7. Nap duck with sauce and serve whole.

Mushrooms, Snow Peas and Bean Sprouts
Serves: 3

Ingredients

4 oz fresh snow peas

3 tablespoons peanut oil

4 oz fresh bean sprouts

4 oz fresh mushrooms, sliced

1 teaspoon soy sauce

Directions

1. Heat the oil in a wok over high heat. Add the mushrooms and snow peas, stir-frying for 3 to 4 minutes until the snow peas are just about tender-crisp.

2. Add the bean sprouts and then stir-fry for at least 30 seconds.

3. Add the soy sauce, stir and serve.

Thai Cabbage Nam Pla
Serves: 4

Ingredients

2 tablespoons Thai fish sauce (nam pla)

2 tablespoons lime juice

2/3 Teaspoon red pepper flakes

1/3 cup unsweetened, flaked coconut

6 cups finely shredded napa cabbage

2 cloves garlic, crushed

6 scallions, sliced

¼ cup chopped, dry-roasted peanuts

Peanut oil

Directions

1. Combine the fish sauce, lime juice and red pepper flakes. Set combination aside.

2. In a wok, heat a few tablespoons of oil over high heat. Now add the scallions, cabbage and garlic and stir-fry 5 minutes.

3. Add the lime juice mixture to it and stir well to coat.

4. Cook 1more minute and then add the coconut, stir and serve topped with peanuts.

Zucchini & Tomato Parmesan

Serves: 6

<u>Ingredients</u>

2 medium zucchini cut lengthwise in two and sliced ¼-inch thick (2½ cups)

4 green onions, (¾ cup), bias-sliced into 1-inch lengths

2 medium tomatoes, seeded &chopped (1 cup)

¼ cup grated Parmesan cheese

1 teaspoon cooking oil

¼ cup snipped parsley

1 clove garlic, minced

<u>Directions</u>

1. Preheat wok and add the cooking oil. Stir-fry the garlic for 15 seconds in hot oil.

2. Add zucchini and stir-fry for 1-2 minutes. Add green onions; stir-fry until vegetables are crisp-tender.

3. Add the parsley and tomatoes. Cover and cook until heated through.

4. Finally, sprinkle with Parmesan cheese; tossing gently.

Spinach and Garlic Chips Sautéed

Serves: 4

Ingredients

4 bunches spinach, washed and dried

1/3 cup extra virgin olive oil

Pinch hot pepper flakes

4 cloves garlic, sliced

Directions

1. Add the oil to a wok over low heat. Add the garlic immediately; do not let the oil heat.

2. Stir fry garlic for about 5 minutes and remove when the chips are brown. Transfer to paper towels to drain.

3. Add the spinach and pepper flakes. Increase heat to medium high and sauté for 3-4 minutes until wilted but not so soft.

4. Sprinkle with garlic chips and serve hot.

Stir-Fried Water Chestnuts And Green Beans

Serves: 3

Ingredients

2 cups frozen green beans, thawed

2 tablespoons oil

½ cup canned water chestnuts, sliced or diced, drained

¼ cup chicken broth

1 clove garlic, crushed

Xanthan or guar

1½ teaspoons soy sauce

Directions

1. Heat the oil wok over high heat.

2. Next, add the water chestnuts and green beans and sauté until the green beans are tender-crisp.

3. Add the soy sauce, garlic and chicken broth, and simmer 2-3 minutes.

4. Thicken the pan juices with a little xanthan or guar and serve.

A Taste Of Fantasy

Serves: 2

<u>Ingredients</u>

12 black mushrooms

1/8 teaspoon five-spice powder

3/4 pound spinach linguine

1 teaspoon distilled wheat mesh

2 teaspoons sugar

1 teaspoon of sesame oil

5 teaspoons cornmeal, un-enriched

Soy sauce

Vegetable oil, for deep frying

Wine

6 oz bean sprouts

1/4 teaspoon fresh black pepper

1 teaspoon white vinegar

2 teaspoons soy sauce paste

Thin slices ginger, soaked in white vinegar and sugar

1/8 teaspoon salt

<u>Directions</u>

1. Soak the mushrooms and remove the stems once soft. Cut mushroom in twirl strips (cut from the outer edge to the center, about 1/2-inch wide).

2. Squeeze excess water out and marinate for 5 minutes with five spice, sugar and salt. After 5 minutes, marinate with wheat mesh, cornmeal, soy sauce, and sesame oil for 30 minutes.

3. Heat vegetable oil in wok until oil is almost smoking. Deep-fry the mushrooms until crispy and remove.

4. Next, deep-fry spinach linguine for 1½ minutes until crispy. Place on dish. Stir-fry the fresh bean sprouts with pepper and wine and place over linguine.

5. Mix vinegar, soy paste, wine and sugar in wok until hot and then add mushrooms and stir thoroughly.

6. Place on top of the linguine and bean sprout. Add ginger as garnish on top.

Broccoli Ginger Stir-Fry
Serves: 4

Ingredients

2 to 3 tablespoons peanut oil

2 cloves garlic, crushed

1 tablespoon fresh ginger, grated

1 bag (1 pound) frozen broccoli "cuts," thawed

1 tablespoon soy sauce

Directions

1. Heat the peanut oil in a wok over high heat. Add the garlic and broccoli until the broccoli is tender crisp.

2. Add the ginger and soy sauce, stir-fry 1 more minute, and then serve.

Spring Scallops And Asparagus

Serves: 2 to 3

Ingredients

10 asparagus spears, sliced diagonally into ½-inch pieces

2 cups bay scallops

2 teaspoons soy sauce

10 scallions, sliced

½ cup carrot, shredded

¼ cup canola oil

Directions

1. Heat the oil in a wok over high heat.

2. Add the asparagus, carrot, scallops and scallions. Stir-fry until the scallops are cooked through and the asparagus is tender-crisp.

3. Stir in the soy sauce and serve.

Chinese Supreme Stock

Yields: 15 cups of stock

This stock is often used in Chinese cooking as soup base, gravies and sauces as well as flavor for vegetable meals. It is often made with chicken, turkey or meat and boiled for at least 4 hours to bring out its flavor.

<u>Ingredients</u>

2 pounds lean pork

1 whole chicken

1 teaspoon salt

Water to cover the ingredients 4 inches and above

<u>Directions</u>

1. Add all the ingredients together in a large stock pot. Do not add the salt.

2. Cook on high and reduce to medium- low and then simmer 3 hours.

3. Add the salt; remove from heat and leave to cool. Remove chicken and pork from stock using a slotted spoon.

4. Divide stock into small containers and chill for 6-9 hours or until the fat solidifies on the stock surface.

5. Remove fat from stock and then freeze the stock in small containers or ice cube trays and store in the freezer for use in the future.

6. The frozen stock can be stored in freezer at least 2 months.

Pea Shoots In Chinese Supreme Stock

Pea shoots are sweet, tender, and high in fiber. Using supreme stock (see above) enhances the flavor of pea shoots. However, chicken broth can also be used.

Serves: 4

Ingredients

1 pound pea shoots

1 teaspoon vegetable oil

2 teaspoons cooking wine

½ teaspoon minced ginger

½ cup Chinese supreme stock or chicken broth

¼ teaspoon salt

1 teaspoon cornstarch

1 red chili pepper, chopped (for garnish, optional)

Pinch of sugar

Directions

1. Heat a wok over high heat. Add the vegetable oil, swirling to coat sides.

2. Next, add ginger and stir until fragrant. Add wine, sugar and pea shoots. Stir-fry about 3 to 5 minutes or until cooked but still green and crisp. Transfer to a serving plate.

3. Place a medium saucepan over medium heat and add stock, cornstarch and salt, stirring frequently.

4. Cook 1 minute to make a thin sauce. Pour the sauce over the pea shoots and then garnish with red pepper.

Asian Eggplant Stir Fry

<u>Ingredients</u>

4 Asian eggplants, sliced diagonally, 1/2-inch thick

5 scallions, cut diagonally in 1 1/2 inches long pieces

2 tablespoons sesame oil

1 tablespoon vegetable oil

1 1/2 cups snow peas

1/4 cup soy sauce cooked rice

2 red peppers, sliced thinly

2 teaspoons dark brown sugar

<u>Directions</u>

1. Heat a wok over medium high heat. Add the oils and heat until almost smoking.

2. Now add the eggplant and peppers. Cook until softened, 4 minutes and then add the snow peas and scallions.

3. Place the soy sauce and sugar in a bowl to dissolve and then add to the wok.

4. Cook for 3 minutes and serve over rice.

Dragon's Fire

So hot, you are literally breathing fire!

Serves: 4

Ingredients

1 head Napa cabbage, cut lengthwise in half & sliced ½-inch thick

¼ cup chili garlic paste

1 teaspoon salt

2 teaspoons Splenda

2 teaspoons toasted sesame oil

2 tablespoons soy sauce

2 tablespoons peanut or canola oil

2 teaspoons rice vinegar

Directions

1. Combine the toasted sesame oil, chili garlic paste, soy sauce, Splenda and salt in a small bowl and set aside.

2. Heat the canola or peanut oil in a wok over highest heat.

3. Add the cabbage and begin to stir-fry. After 1minute or so, add the seasoning mixture and continue to stir-fry until the cabbage just begins to wilt.

4. Add the rice vinegar, stir again, and serve.

SEAFOOD RECIPES

Wok-Seared Shrimp
Serves: 4

Ingredients

1/2 cup reduced-sodium chicken broth

3 pounds large or jumbo shrimp, peeled & deveined

8 oz cellophane noodles

2 teaspoons cornstarch

2 tablespoons reduced-sodium soy sauce

1 teaspoon red pepper flakes, crushed

1 tablespoon fresh ginger, minced

1 tablespoon peanut or vegetable oil

1/4 cup scallions, chopped

4 cloves garlic, minced

Directions

1. Soak the cellophane noodles for 10 minutes in hot water until it's soft. Drain and set aside.

2. Meanwhile, whisk together red pepper flakes, soy sauce, broth and cornstarch in a small bowl. Set aside.

3. Heat oil in a wok over medium-high heat. Add garlic and ginger and cook for 1 minute.

4. Add shrimp and cook until pink (2 to 3 minutes). Add the broth mixture and cook for 1 minute.

5. Remove from heat, add the scallions and stir. Serve just half of the shrimp over the cellophane noodles but include all the sauce.

6. Reserve the rest of the shrimp for shrimp cakes, if desired.

Orange Steamed Fish
Serves: 2

Ingredients

1 lb. fish fillets (scrod or cod

1 med. onion, chopped

2 tbsp. cooking oil

Hot cooked rice

1/2 tsp. grated ginger root

2 cloves garlic, minced

1/4 cup frozen orange juice concentrate

1 tbsp. soy sauce

2 tbsp. snipped parsley

1/8 tsp. pepper

Directions

1. Arrange the fish in a heatproof dish. Heat the wok over high heat and then add oil.

2. Stir-fry ginger root, onion and garlic in hot oil for about 5 minutes. Stir in soy sauce, juice concentrate, pepper and parsley and bring to a boil. Pour this mixture over fish.

3. Wipe out the wok dry. Add water to it and heat the water to boiling (let it reach 1/2 inch below the steamer rack).

4. Place the serving dish with fish on steamer rack (leave some holes open to allow steam to circulate).

5. Cover and steam until fish flakes when tested with a fork, about 10 minutes.

 Serve with hot cooked rice.

Sweet Saigon Shrimp

Serves: 4

Ingredients

1 pound large shrimp, shelled& deveined

3 scallions, sliced thinly

1½ teaspoons chili garlic paste

1½ teaspoons Splenda

2 teaspoons minced garlic

¼ cup peanut or canola oil

½ teaspoon salt

½ teaspoon pepper

Directions

1. In a small dish, combine the Splenda, salt and pepper.

2. Heat the oil in a wok over highest heat, add the shrimp and stir-fry it 2 to 3 minutes. Add the garlic and chili garlic paste and stir-fry continuously.

3. Once the shrimp are all pink, add the Splenda, salt and pepper mixture and stir 10-15 seconds.

4. Turn off heat and serve the shrimp top with sliced scallion.

Woked Dungeness Crab

Serves: 6

<u>Ingredients</u>

1 tablespoon of cornstarch mixed with 2 tablespoons of water

1 pound Dungeness or jumbo lump crabmeat, cleaned

1 cup fermented black beans, rinsed

4 Dungeness crabs, (1½ pounds each) cleaned &broken into pieces

1/2 cup cilantro leaves, chopped

2 tablespoons lime juice

1/2 cup chopped green onions

1 1/2 cups fish stock

1/2 cup sherry

1/4 cup dark soy sauce

1/4 cup chopped cashews

1/4 cup peanut oil

2 -inch piece fresh ginger, grated

5 garlic cloves, chopped

1 Thai chili pepper, minced

6 heads baby bok choy, halved &steamed

<u>Directions</u>

1. Combine cilantro, soy, fish stock, green onions, lime juice, black beans, sherry and cashews in a skillet. Simmer until sauce begins to thicken.

2. Next, add the crabmeat and the cornstarch mixture and cook 1 minute.

3. Meanwhile, add the peanut oil in a wok over high heat. Once peanut oil is hot, add the crab pieces, garlic, chili, ginger and stir-fry 3 to 4 minutes.

4. Top crab pieces with sauce and steamed bok choy on the side. Enjoy!

Chinese Stir-Fried Shark

Serves: 4

Ingredients

3 tablespoon of salad oil

1 tbsp. minced fresh ginger

1 to 1 1/4 lbs. boned shark, cut in 1 inch chunks

2 cup thin, diagonal slices celery

1 pkg. (3 oz.) dry Ramen noodles (remove seasoning packet)

3 cup edible pea pods, ends & strings removed

2 tablespoon each oriental sesame oil & soy sauce

1/4 cup seasoned rice vinegar

1/4 cup cilantro (coriander) sprigs

Directions

1. Place 2 tablespoon of salad oil in a wok over medium high heat.

2. Add ginger and fish; stir fry 4 to 6 minutes until fish is a little translucent but it still moist in center. Remove from wok and set aside.

3. Add the remaining 1 tbsp salad oil, peas and celery to wok. Stir-fry 4 to 5 minutes until veggies are tender-crisp. Remove from heat.

4. Add fish, sesame oil, vinegar cilantro, soy, noodles (broken into bite-size pieces) and stir gently.

Shrimp Pad Thai

Serves: 2

Ingredients

1 pound shrimp, peeled & deveined

8 oz flat rice noodles

4 ounces basil leaves, stems removed

Olive oil

2 eggs, beaten

4 ounces firm tofu, cubed

2 cloves garlic, minced

1/2 cup fish sauce

1/2 teaspoon habenero pepper, minced

3 tablespoons brown sugar

1/2 cup bean sprouts

2 tablespoons lightly salted peanuts, finely chopped

2 limes, cut into wedges

1/ cup mint leaves

Directions

1. For the noodles, soften it in water as instructed on package. Drain and set aside.

2. For the Pad Thai, heat the wok over high heat and add 2 tablespoons oil. Once the oil starts to shimmer, add the basil and fry until crisp. Remove basil to a paper towel.

3. Add 1 tablespoon of oil to the wok, add tofu and stir-fry about 2 minutes. Scramble the eggs quickly to it. Transfer to a plate and dry the wok with a clean cloth.

4. Heat the wok and add the 2 tablespoons of oil that is left. When oil is hot, add the habanera pepper and garlic and cook 20 seconds.

5. Add the fish sauce and then add the brown sugar. Let it heat through and then add the noodles. Toss to let the noodles absorb most of the sauce.

6. Finally, add the reserved tofu, peanuts, shrimp, bean sprouts, and eggs. Toss and remove to a serving platter.

7. Garnish dish with lime, mint and basil.

Fish Bundles And Broccoli
Serves: 4

4 fresh or frozen fish fillets

(10 oz.) 1 pkg. frozen broccoli spears

2 small carrots, quartered lengthwise

1/2 teaspoon dried dill weed

1 tablespoon butter

2 lemon slices, halved

1/4 cup mayonnaise

1/4 cup whipping cream

1/4 teaspoon salt

Directions

1. If fish is frozen, thaw. Pour small amount of water in a saucepan and add the carrots and broccoli, boiling until crisp-tender; drain.

2. Next, dot the fish fillets with butter and sprinkle with salt and dill. Place carrots and broccoli across fish fillets; roll fish up around veggies and hold securely with wooden picks.

3. Pour boiling water into wok (let it reach 1/2 inch below the steamer rack). Arrange fish fillets on rack topped with a half lemon slice each.

4. Cover wok and steam for 12 to 15 minutes.

5. Meanwhile, whip cream until it forms soft peaks; fold in mayonnaise. Pass the sauce with fish.

Orange Roughy Stir Fry

Serves: 6

Ingredients

2 tablespoon cornstarch

3 orange roughy fillets

4 tablespoon corn oil

2 carrots, chopped

2 green onion, chopped

2 sticks of celery chopped

Sauce:

1/2 cup chicken broth

1 tsp. cornstarch

1 tbsp. soy sauce

1 tbsp. rice wine

Directions

1. Cut each of the roughy fillet into 4 pieces and coat them all with 1 tablespoon of oil.

2. Next, sprinkle cornstarch over the fish. Roll the fish over many times until cornstarch and oil dissolve. Let it stand for about 30 minutes.

3. Heat 2 tablespoon of corn oil in the wok. Cook four pieces of fish at a time. Transfer to a hot plate. When all fish is cooked, add 1 tablespoon of oil, add carrots and stir for 1 minute.

4. Add celery and onion. Keep stir frying and put fish back in wok. Empty the sauce over fish and veggies.

5. Once the sauce thickens, remove to a hot platter. Serve with steamed rice.

Wok-Cooked Mussels
Serves: 2

Ingredients

1/2 pound mussels

1 tablespoon minced garlic

1/2 glass white wine

1/4 cup butter

1/2 pint heavy cream

Thyme, to taste

1/4 cup water

Directions

1. In a wok over medium heat, place the water and mussels. Once they start opening, strain out the water.

2. Now add the white wine. Cook out the alcohol and once it starts boiling, add the butter, cream, garlic and thyme.

3. Lower heat and serve when the mussels have all opened. Discard the unopened mussels, if any.

Mock-Style Lobster
Serves: 3

Ingredients

1 1/2 lbs. white fish (turbot, cod)

1/4 cup cooking oil

2 pieces ginger (1/2 dollar size, 1/4 inch thick)

1 bunch green onions

1 clove garlic

2 cup water

Directions

1. Slice fish filets into pieces (diagonally, 1 inch wide and thick) and place in a heatproof pan.

2. Dice ginger, green onion tops and garlic. Sprinkle over fish.

3. Pour water in a wok to just below steam level and heat to boiling. Place the fish pan in the wok on steam rack and cover.

4. Once fish is solid white, heat the oil to smoking point. Take out excess liquid from the fish pan and pour hot oil quickly over fish. Dip fish in melted butter.

Sautéed Seafood With Asparagus

Serves: 4

Ingredients:

1 bunch of thin asparagus, cut in 2 inches lengths (discard bottom fourth)

1 medium- sized onion, cut in half & sliced medium thick

8 large scallops

1 tablespoon chicken or vegetable broth

3 medium garlic cloves, chopped

1 tablespoon minced fresh ginger

2 cups fresh sliced shiitake mushrooms

1/4 cup of fresh lemon juice

2 tablespoon mirin wine

2 tablespoon soy sauce

3/4 lb cod fillet cut into 1 inch pieces

8 large shrimp, peeled& deveined

1 cup cherry tomatoes cut in quarters

1/4 cup fresh cilantro, chopped

Salt& white pepper to taste

Pinch red pepper flakes

Directions:

1. Chop garlic and slice onion and let sit for 5 to10 minutes.

2. Heat 1 tablespoon of broth in a wok.

3. Sauté onion in broth for 2 minutes over medium high heat, stirring often. Add garlic, ginger, asparagus and mushrooms. Keep stir-frying for 3 more minutes, stirring often.

4. Add soy sauce, lemon juice, mirin, cod, red pepper flakes, shrimp and scallops and stir, mixing well.

5. Cover and simmer 5 minutes, stirring on medium heat occasionally.

6. Toss in cilantro, tomatoes, salt and pepper. Enjoy!

Stir-Fry Chili Seafood
Serves: 4

<u>Ingredients</u>

600 g scallops, no roe

500 g uncooked medium king prawns

1/2 teaspoon five-spice powder

1/2 teaspoon black pepper

2 red Thai chile, finely chopped

2 garlic cloves, crushed

2 tablespoons peanut oil

1 1/2 teaspoons ginger

1 small red pepper

120 g bean sprouts

1 small yellow pepper

12 baby asparagus spears

2 -3 tablespoons light soy sauce

150 g sugar snap peas

1 -2 teaspoon sugar

2 tablespoons fresh chives, chopped finely

Directions

1. In a bowl, combine seafood, chili, five-spice, garlic, pepper and ginger.

2. Heat half of the oil in a wok and stir-fry seafood in batches. Remove once cooked.

3. Heat the remaining oil in wok and stir-fry peppers until tender. Add asparagus, peas and sprouts to wok, stir-fry 1 minute.

4. Return the seafood to wok; add sugar and soy sauce, stir-fry until hot.

5. Add just 1 tablespoon of chopped chives and sprinkle the rest over dishes.

Stir-Fried Seafood Pasta
Serves: 8

Ingredients:

1 pound medium pasta (bow ties or radiator),uncooked

2 tablespoons white wine vinegar

2 cloves garlic, minced

2 tablespoons reduced-sodium soy sauce

2 teaspoons minced fresh ginger

8 ounces fresh snow peas, cut in half

1/4 cup fresh orange juice

8 ounces sea scallops

1 tablespoon grated orange peel

8 ounces, peeled &deveined, uncooked shrimp

1 tablespoon vegetable oil

2 carrots, julienned

2 teaspoons corn starch

1 red bell pepper, ribs and seeds removed, julienned

1 tablespoon water

1/2 teaspoon hot red pepper flakes (optional)

Directions

1. Add together vinegar, garlic, ginger, orange juice, soy sauce and orange peel in a bowl.

2. Add scallops and shrimp and gently toss to coat seafood. Cover and chill 30 minutes, stirring from time to time.

3. Cook pasta as instructed in the package. Meanwhile, heat oil in wok; add the shrimp mixture but do not drain.

4. If using, add the hot red pepper flakes and stir-fry 2 minutes. Now add snow peas, bell pepper and carrots; cover and cook 2 minutes.

5. Add water to cornstarch to dissolve, stir into wok and cook 1 minute.

6. Once pasta is cooked, drain well. Remove to serving platter and pour stir-fry over it. Toss lightly.

Sweet Spicy Wok With Norwegian Salmon

Serves: 4

Ingredients

2 portion instant ramen noodles

4 each 5-6 oz Norwegian Salmon fillets

200 g snow peas

1 piece bell peppers, red

1 tbsp canola oil

6 tbsp sweet chili sauce

2 tbsp Soy Sauce

10 leaves cilantro, fresh

1 lime

Directions

1. Cook noodles following the instructions on the package. Cut salmon in 3 cm pieces. Also cut the sugar peas and paprika.

2. Fry salmon in oil 1-2 minutes per side pale pink in color. Remove from the wok and reserve.

3. Fry the veggies on high heat and then juice the lime. Now add the sweet chili sauce, limejuice, soy sauce and boiled noodles to the veggies.

4. Heat the sauce and add the salmon. Serve.

MISCELLANEOUS RECIPES

Rice In Wok
Yield: 3 cups of rice

<u>Ingredients</u>

2 cups of water

1 cup of rice

<u>Directions</u>

1. Bring water to a boil in a wok on high heat. Add rice, stir and cover.

2. Lower heat to medium; simmer until water is completely or about 15 minutes.

3. Turn heat off and let rice sit for 5 minutes. Fluff with fork and serve

Frozen Tofu In Stock

The texture of the tofu becomes meaty and spongy when frozen.

Serves: 4

Ingredients:

6 dried shiitake mushrooms, soaked, stems removed

4 pieces 2 by 2 inches firm tofu (frozen 8 hours beforehand or overnight)

16 slices of extra lean, 2 inches x 2 inches ham (about 5 oz in total weight)

1 cup of low sodium chicken broth or supreme stock (see *table of content*)

2 cups of broccoli florets

4 cups water

Sauce:

1½ teaspoons soy sauce

2 teaspoons cornstarch

1 teaspoon sugar

Pinch of white pepper

½ teaspoon sesame seed oil

Directions

1. Place frozen tofu under running tap water to defrost and then squeeze out excess water. Cut each tofu into 4 pieces of ½ inch thickness to total 16 slices.

2. Place tofu and ham around the sides of a large bowl in an overlapping pattern. Place the mushrooms in the center and then pour in the broth.

3. Bring water to a boil in a wok. Put a steamer rack above the water and place the bowl with tofu, mushrooms and ham on the rack. Cover and steam 20 minutes over high heat, then remove.

4. Drain broth from bowl into a medium sized pan. Cook stock over medium heat, add the sauce ingredients and stir continuously to make light gravy.

5. Next, cover the steamed tofu bowl with a large plate, invert the bowl onto plate, and then remove the bowl.

6. Heat 4 cups water in a medium sized; bring to boil over high heat. Place steamer rack into pot and add broccoli. Cover pot and steam for 4-5 minutes over medium heat.

7. Garnish tofu and ham with broccoli, pour the gravy on top and serve.

French- Styled Onion Soup

Serves: 4-6

Ingredients

6 medium brown onions, finely sliced

2 tablespoons of all purpose flour

2 tablespoons butter

1 tablespoon oil

1 clove of garlic, crushed

1 teaspoon chopped fresh thyme

1 tablespoon brown sugar

1 cup red wine

4½ cups beef stock

Directions

1. Set wok to high. Add the oil, garlic, butter and onions and stir-fry until onions is golden in color.

2. Add the flour, cook 1 minute, add the wine and thyme and let the liquid reduce by half.

3. Add the brown sugar and beef stock and bring soup to a boil.

4. Lower heat; simmer soup for 30 minutes. If desired, season with salt and pepper and serve with cheese croutons.

Penne With Ham And Cheese

Serves: 4

Ingredients

200 g cubes of smoked bacon

400 g penne

2 cloves of garlic, finely chopped

3 tbsp peanut oil

1 mozzarella, cut into blocks

100g Parmesan, grated

Small handful basil, roughly chopped

Directions

1. Pour a large quantity of water in the wok and bring to boil. Cook penne according to package instruction until al dente. Drain pasta.

2. Wipe wok dry and heat on high. Add the peanut oil, and stir-fry the garlic and bacon about 1 minute.

3 Add the penne and then the mozzarella and Parmesan, mixing well.

4. Let it heat thoroughly for a few minutes. Serve garnished with the basil.

The End

21158047R00068

Printed in Great Britain
by Amazon